# At the museum

## i-SPY

# INTRODUCTION

Welcome to the wonderful world of the museum. Boring and dusty? Definitely not!

Museums do have displays in glass cases but they also have interactive screens, things to try out, try on, or even go inside. There are museums in lots of places too. Small, local museums show exciting archaeological finds from prehistory or Roman times and have displays or exhibitions on how your local area developed. Big city museums often specialize in areas such as transport, natural history or science. So if there is something you are particularly interested in you can choose one of those to visit. You can also visit outdoor living museums where whole buildings have been moved to recreate a village or a mine and you can see how people used to work, play, learn and eat. Dress up and experience school Victorian style, or see how a dentist extracted teeth!

This i-SPY book gives some suggestions for the many different types of museums you can visit. Then you can use it as you explore the different areas in the museum. Find where the displays are that you are interested in or even better discover something new. Museums can be big so you may not see everything on your first visit but that is good news, it means you can go back again. Also while you are visiting look out for posters as there may be a special exhibition area that is used for touring displays.

## How to use your i-SPY book

As you work through this book, you will notice that the subjects are arranged in groups which are related to the kinds of places where you are likely to find things. You need 1000 points to send off for your i-SPY certificate (see page 64) but that is not too difficult because there are masses of points in every book. Each entry has a star or circle and points value beside it. The stars represent harder to spot entries. As you make each i-SPY, write your score in the circle or star. There are questions dotted throughout the book that can double your i-SPY score. Check your answers on page 63.

*There are many different types of museum. Some are dedicated to one particular subject, while others may hold a variety of collections. See if the museum you are visiting fits one or more of these descriptions.*

## NATURAL HISTORY

**Points: 20**

Plants, animals, insects, marine creatures and fossils tell the story of the varied and changing environments in this country and beyond.

**Points: 25**

## ARTS

The arts includes design, film, media and all forms of art such as painting and drawing, sculpture, ceramics, textile art and glasswork.

## MILITARY AND WAR

**Points: 25**

The history of the armed forces and the conflicts in which they have fought are depicted in various museums around the country. Some are based at centres of operations or intelligence, or even on old war ships.

### TRANSPORT

The many and varied types of transport that have been used for different purposes over the years are displayed in museums around the country.

**Points: 15**

### SCIENCE AND TECHNOLOGY

Many of these museums have interactive displays and hands-on exhibits where you can learn all about the technology we use and the science behind it.

**Points: 20**

### HERITAGE AND INDUSTRY

The cultural, industrial or social history of a particular place is often preserved in a local heritage centre.

**Points: 15**

### MULTIPLE COLLECTIONS

Some museums contain more than one type of collection, perhaps arranged over different floors of the building.

**Points: 10**

### MARITIME

Several ports around the country have collections illustrating the history of sailing in this seafaring nation.

*Score double points for a museum on a ship.*

 **Points: 25**

### SPECIALIST

Whether it is dedicated to a particular sport, slavery, lawnmowers, witchcraft or waxworks, score points if the museum you are visiting is the only one – or is among just a few of its kind – in the country.

**Points: 20**

### HISTORIC HOUSE

Historic houses could be grand stately homes or the former homes of famous people, usually preserved as they were when the person lived there.

**Points: 10**

### LOCAL INTEREST

All kinds of exhibits relating to the local area may be gathered together into a single museum.

**Points: 15**

### CAFÉ

**Points: 10**

You can spend all day at a museum if it has a café where you can buy a drink and a sandwich at lunchtime.

 **Points: 5**

### SOUVENIR SHOP

Nearly every museum has a shop selling books, toys, pictures and souvenirs to remind you of your visit.

### DONATION BOX

**Points: 10**

Look out for these near the entrance. Many museums are free to enter and rely on visitors to donate money towards their running costs.

### Points: 10

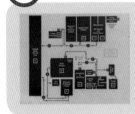

Check the layout of the museum to see where you want to go first and also to make sure you don't miss anything out.

 **Points: 20**

If you have a large bag with you it is handy to be able to store it away in a locker while you look around the museum.

### Points: 10

This is useful for people in pushchairs or wheelchairs, or if your legs are too tired to climb the stairs.

## INTERACTIVE DISPLAY

**Points: 5**

Look out for touchscreen displays where you can look up information, complete quizzes and play games.

**Points: 10**

## DISCOVERY TRAIL

Ask at the information desk if there is a discovery trail where you have to hunt for items or answer questions as you look around the museum.

## COLOURING IN

**Points: 10**

Look out for a table with paper and pencils for drawing. There may be pictures of exhibits for you to colour in.

 **Points: 30**

**FILM THEATRE**

Bigger museums may have a theatre or IMAX cinema showing all sorts of films.

**LIVING DISPLAY**

**Points: 40**

At some museums you will see people demonstrating how we used to live or work in the past, dressed in the clothing of the time.

Martin Charles Hatch / Shutterstock.com

9

*Plants or animals that died millions of years ago often became embedded into rock as it formed. They tell us a lot about prehistoric life on Earth. See if you can find these types of fossils.*

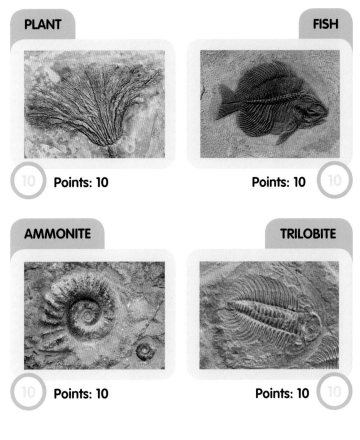

**PLANT**

Points: 10

**FISH**

Points: 10

**AMMONITE**

Points: 10

**TRILOBITE**

Points: 10

**Points: 10**

## BUTTERFLY

There are over 18,000 species of butterflies around the world, some of which are very colourful. You may find a tray or drawer in the museum showing several different types.

## SEASHELL

**Points: 5**

Shells are the protective outer layer of marine creatures, and are often washed up on the beach after the creature dies.

**Points: 5**

## BIRD'S EGG

Birds lay their eggs in all sorts of different nests, from a sandy patch on the ground to a woven basket of twigs high up in a tree.

*Score double points if the egg is in a nest.*

## ANIMAL SKULL

**Points: 15**

It can be very difficult to identify an animal from just its skull, though the horns on this one give you a clue.

**Points: 25**

## DINOSAUR SKELETON

Whole dinosaur skeletons show just how big and scary these creatures must have been!

## DIPPY THE DIPLODOCUS

Points: 50  Top Spot!  50

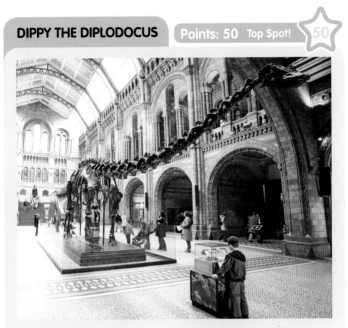

For more than 100 years the Natural History Museum in London exhibited this life size replica of a diplodocus skeleton. Affectionately known as 'Dippy' it was moved to the central hall of the museum in 1979 making it one of the first things visitors would see when they arrived. Its sheer size, at over 21 metres (69 ft) long and 4 metres high (13 ft), made this popular exhibit impossible to miss, but in 2016 it was decided that it was time for a change and Dippy would be replaced by the skeleton of a blue whale. However, if you've never seen him, fear not, because like the star he is Dippy is going on tour and will spend the next few years travelling to museums all over the country.

## SEED

**Points: 15**   15

Seeds can vary in size from almost microscopic to absolutely enormous!

5   **Points: 5**

## GEMSTONE

You will find these in the geology section. They are types of rock but are so pretty that they are often used to make jewellery.

**Points: 20**
double with answer   20

## TREE RINGS

You can tell how old a tree is by counting the rings that are shown on a cross section of the trunk. Rings will vary in thickness depending on the weather conditions that year.

*What is the practice of counting tree rings called?*

*Taxidermy is the art of stuffing animals that have died. This preserves them in three-dimensional form, and allows us to examine animals that are difficult to see in the wild.*

**FISH**

Points: 10

**BIRD**

Points: 5

**MAMMAL**

Points: 5

**EXTINCT SPECIES**

Points: 30

## LADY'S LONG DRESS

**Points: 20**

Until about 1925 it was considered unacceptable for women to show their legs, so they always wore long skirts and dresses.

**Points: 15**

## SUIT OF ARMOUR

Metal armour was developed in the Middle Ages to protect soldiers – and sometimes their horses – during battle. It was very heavy, and restricted the soldiers' movements.

## PAIR OF SHOES

**Points: 10**

Primitive shoes were made of animal fur, leaves or bark. Nowadays we have lots of different styles of footwear for all our different activities.

## Points: 15

Historically the soldiers of the English army wore red, but the British Army has adopted khaki for its combat uniforms as this provides better camouflage.

## Points: 15

Navy uniforms have changed over the years and also vary according to the rank and job of the person wearing them.

## Points: 40

These feathered war bonnets are traditionally worn by the male leaders of native American Indian tribes. Only those who have earned the right may wear them as they have a great spiritual importance. Score points for any feathered headdress.

## SPACE SUIT

**Points: 20**
double with answer

Astronauts need to wear these specially designed suits to protect them from the harsh environment in space.

*Who was the first person to walk on the moon?*

**Points: 10**

HAT

Score points for any type of hat you see, whether it is a military cap, a fez, a lady's hat or a sombrero!

## MINER'S HELMET

**Points: 20**

Hard hats protect miners' heads from falling rocks, and the lights on the front help them to see in the dark mines.

## Points: 15

### RADIO

Before televisions became available, people used to rely on the radio (or 'wireless') to listen to news, music and entertainment. The first regular broadcasts were made in the 1920s.

### TELEPHONE

## Points: 10

Telephone technology has come a long way since the first telephone calls were made in the 1870s. This 'rotary' style of telephone became popular in the middle of the last century.

## Points: 30

### BLACK AND WHITE TELEVISION

Until about 1970 most people's televisions showed pictures in black and white rather than colour.

## CLOCK

**Points: 10**

Before mechanical clocks were invented in the Middle Ages, people used sundials, candles and hourglasses to measure time. Score points for any time-keeping device.

**Points: 30**

## MAGIC LANTERN

This very early type of projector originally showed films made of images painted onto glass slides.

## BOX CAMERA

**Points: 25**

These early cameras had a simple design, with a lens at one end and the film at the other.

**Points: 20**

## GRAMOPHONE

This old name for a record player is mostly associated with these wind-up machines. They were very popular in the early 1900s.

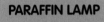

## PARAFFIN LAMP

**Points: 25**

Before people had electric lights in their homes, paraffin lamps provided a safer and brighter source of light than candles.

**Points: 20**

## KITCHEN APPLIANCE

The increasing supply of electricity to homes in the 1940s and 1950s led to a revolution in appliances to help in the kitchen. Score points for any electrical appliance.

## MICROSCOPE

**Points: 10**

With a microscope it is possible to see things that are too small to be seen by the naked human eye. They are also used for examining small objects in fine detail.

**Points: 15**

## TELESCOPE

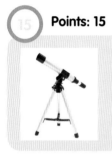

Optical telescopes use lenses to allow us to see distant objects more clearly. They were developed by astronomers who wanted to know more about the night sky.

## STETHOSCOPE

**Points: 30**

Medicine makes good use of technology. A stethoscope is a simple device that allows a doctor to listen to a patient's heartbeat.

**Points: 50**  Top Spot!

### ROBOT

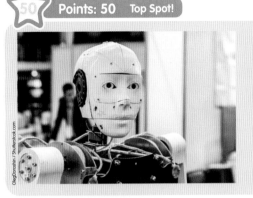

Robots are machines that are programmed to carry out tasks automatically. They are used a lot in manufacturing and engineering.

### FLIGHT SIMULATOR

**Points: 50**  Top Spot!

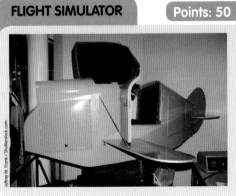

Take control of an aeroplane, helicopter or rocket in a flight simulator to experience the thrill of flying.

### RATION BOOK
**Points: 15**

Food was in short supply during the First and Second World Wars so certain things had to be sold in strictly measured amounts to those people who had the correct ration book.

**Points: 15**

### GAS MASK

These are used to protect people from poisonous gasses. During World War Two, all civilians and soldiers were issued with their own mask.

### CAMPAIGN MAP
**Points: 15**

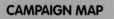

Maps were used in planning and recording military campaigns.

**50** Points: 50 Top Spot!

## CODEBREAKING MACHINE

These machines allowed enemy messages that were sent in special code to be deciphered.

## REGIMENTAL CAP BADGE

Points: 10 10

Each regiment of the British Army has its own distinguishing badge that the soldiers wear on their caps. Have a go at designing your own badge.

**5** Points: 5
double with answer

## MEDAL

Medals are awarded to servicemen and women for service, conduct and bravery.

*What is the name of the highest award in the British military?*

*How many of these vehicles used by the military can you spot?*

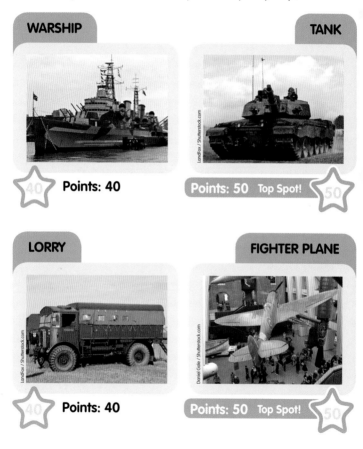

**WARSHIP**

**Points: 40**

**TANK**

**Points: 50** Top Spot!

**LORRY**

**Points: 40**

**FIGHTER PLANE**

**Points: 50** Top Spot!

Points: 5

Statues are usually of people or animals. They are life-sized or bigger and made of stone, metal or wood.

VASE

Points: 10

Different cultures and civilisations had their own ways of making and decorating vases.

Points: 10

BUST

A bust is a statue that shows just the head and neck, and sometimes also the shoulders.

Points: 25

Glass beads were first made thousands of years ago and were used for jewellery and decoration. In some countries they were used as an early form of currency.

Points: 20

STAINED GLASS

Stained glass is mostly used in church windows and looks beautiful with the light shining through.

**Points: 25**

Large tapestry wall hangings often depict stories or scenes from history. They would take hours of intricate needlework to complete, but added warmth and colour to draughty houses.

Jörg Hackemann / Shutterstock.com

**Points: 15**

Look out for collections of photographs on a particular theme, sometimes as part of a temporary exhibition or competition.

Adriano Castelli / Shutterstock.com

## PAINTING

There are many styles of painting, and different types of paint can be used to create different effects.

Popova Valeriya / Shutterstock.com

**Points: 20**

## FILM REEL

Films (as in movies) take their name from the reels of film that are run through a projector, which in turn projects the image onto a big screen for viewing.

## CLAPPERBOARD

**Points: 20**

PRODUCTION

DIRECTOR

CAMERA

DATE    SCENE    TAKE

Before a scene from a movie is shot, the director shouts 'Action!' and the hinged clapstick on the clapperboard is snapped shut.

Before television the main form of advertising in Britain was in print or on billboards. The messages were usually a lot simpler and to the point than those we see today. You'll see poster adverts in art and media museums, but you'll also find them in transport museums, where they might be advertising popular destinations, or in museums which recreate life in days gone by. Score for any poster advert from any kind of museum.

## MUSICAL INSTRUMENT

**Points: 30**

You may see a musical instrument that belonged to a famous musician.

*Score double points if it is signed by the musician.*

 **Points: 20**

## SIGNED PHOTOGRAPH

Famous actors, sportsmen and women, and television personalities often use signed photographs for publicity.

## VINYL RECORD

**Points: 20**

Music recordings used to be sold on black vinyl discs that were played on a gramophone or record player.

50 **Points: 50** Top Spot!

## STAGE COSTUME

Look out for fancy costumes that famous singers or performers wore on stage.

## TICKET

**Points: 25** 25

CONCERT
"KISS"
CAPITAL CENTRE
SUN JULY 8.1979

capital centre K 883181

enter portal

25062315.15    8:00
16  ADULT.
126
126  -0  11  $ 11.00
SEC  ROW  SEAT  TAX INCL.

Tickets to a music show or sports event can become valuable collector's items.

## SPORTING EQUIPMENT

Points: 25

This includes bats, balls and other equipment used in big sporting events or by famous sportsmen and women.

Points: 25

## GOLD DISC

When musicians sell a certain number of records they are awarded a gold disc. This will be printed with the name of the song or album and the artist who performed it.

*See if you can spot any of these things that help on a journey.*

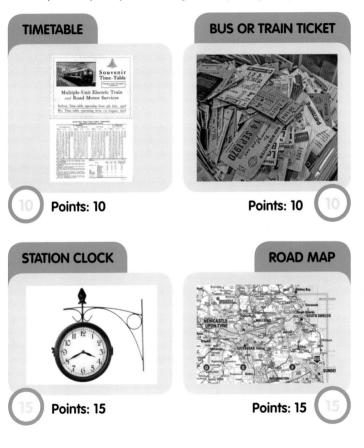

**TIMETABLE**

Points: 10

**BUS OR TRAIN TICKET**

Points: 10

**STATION CLOCK**

Points: 15

**ROAD MAP**

Points: 15

## BUS

**Points: 10**

Eclectic Art and Photography / Shutterstock.com

The term 'bus' is shortened from omnibus, which means 'for all'. Buses provide transport for everyone, which is why they are so big.

 **Points: 15**

### FARM VEHICLE

No farmer would be without a tractor. See if you can spot any other types of farm vehicle too.

SergeyPhoto7 / Shutterstock.com

### HORSE-DRAWN CARRIAGE

**Points: 15**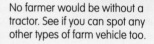

PlusONE / Shutterstock.com

Journeys used to take a lot longer when people travelled by horse-drawn carriage, and they weren't very comfortable for those who had to sit on top!

**Points: 20**

## TRAM CAR

Trams are like a cross between a bus and a train. They usually operate around city centres and run along rails embedded into the road.

## PENNY FARTHING

**Points: 25**

These old bicycles were popular during Victorian times and take their name from two coins of the time, a penny being much larger than a farthing.

**Points: 30**

## TRACTION ENGINE

These steam-powered vehicles became popular from the 1850s. Although they are heavy and slow they are very powerful and provided an alternative to horse-drawn vehicles.

## MOTORBIKE AND SIDECAR

**Points: 40**

A sidecar attached to a motorbike allows a passenger to ride in slightly more comfort than they would be on the back of the bike.

**Points: 40**

## VINTAGE CAR

A car is classed as Vintage if it was built between 1919 and 1930. During this period, cars were becoming much more comfortable to drive in.

## VETERAN CAR

**Points: 50** Top Spot!

Veteran cars are the oldest type of car, built before 1905. At this time cars were being made in the USA and various countries in Europe, including the UK.

## RACING CAR

**Points: 30**

The design of racing cars varies according to the terrain they are racing on so you might see a rally car or even a dragster alongside a Formula One car like the one shown here and you can score for any type you spot. If you do see a Formula One car in a museum it might well be quite a different shape from those you see racing today. This is because the sport has seen many innovations over the years as each team tries to gain more speed. Cars of the 1950s had engines at the front, the 60s introduced 'wings' to help downforce, whereas in the 70s they even tried having 6 wheels!

39

**Points: 10**

It is possible to see how much an area has changed over time by looking at an old map and comparing it with a recent one.

**Points: 10**

SEPIA PHOTOGRAPH

Old monochrome photographs that have a brownish tint were treated with ink from a cuttlefish, which helped to make them last longer.

AERIAL PHOTOGRAPH

**Points: 10**

Photographs taken from the air show you a different view of the area. They are also used by historians and archaeologists to see patterns on the ground that may be the buried ruins of old buildings.

### Points: 10

Local news, opinions and rumours have been reported in newspapers for over three hundred years.

### FAMILY TREE

### Points: 25

The generations of a local family may be illustrated in a family tree, which shows the relationships between the family members.

### Points: 15

### COAT OF ARMS

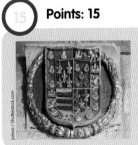

The design of a coat of arms is personal to the individual or family that holds it, though it always includes a shield, supporters, a crest and a motto.

## SCALE MODEL OF A BUILDING

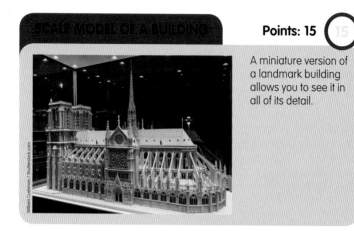

A miniature version of a landmark building allows you to see it in all of its detail.

## ARCHAEOLOGICAL FIND

Archaeological digs can tell us a lot about the history of an area. Smaller finds are often displayed in the local museum.

## BOARD GAME

**Points: 20**

Generations of families have enjoyed playing board games together.

**Points: 15**

## SHEET OF MUSIC

You may see a sheet of music propped up on a piano.

## MODEL RAILWAY

**Points: 40**

Electric model railways have been available since the beginning of the last century. Some models have whole landscapes constructed around them, with lots of detail.

## CHESS SET

**Points: 25**

The game of chess was invented about 1500 years ago. The standard chess pieces are usually made of wood though some sets are elaborately carved from stone or cast in metal.

**Points: 20**

## STAMP COLLECTION

There are so many stamps issued around the world that some stamp collections are very large and valuable.

*Score double points for a Penny Black, the world's first adhesive postage stamp.*

## KIT MODEL

**Points: 20**

Military aircraft and ships are popular subjects for model-makers of all ages, who use kits to build and paint the replica vehicles.

*Look out for these toys, which have been favourites with children for many years.*

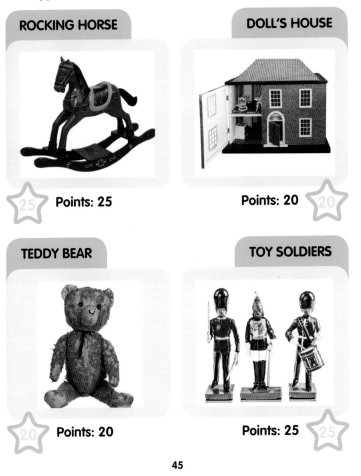

## ROCKING HORSE

**Points: 25**

## DOLL'S HOUSE

**Points: 20**

## TEDDY BEAR

**Points: 20**

## TOY SOLDIERS

**Points: 25**

## SCALE MODEL OF A SHIP

**Points: 15**

Peter Jurca / Shutterstock.com

Score points for any type of seagoing vessel that you see a scaled-down replica of.

**Points: 15**

## NAVIGATION CHART

For centuries mariners have been mapping the seas and coastlines in order to navigate their way safely and accurately.

## SHIP'S BELL

**Points: 25**

Philip Bird LRPS CPAGB / Shutterstock.com

A ship's bell is rung to indicate the time, so that sailors know when to start and end their watch. It is usually engraved with the name of the ship.

**Points: 30**

## LOBSTER POT

These baskets are used by fishermen to catch lobsters in the sea. The lobsters are lured in by bait but are then unable to get out through the narrow opening.

## ROPE LADDER

**Points: 15**

Rope ladders are used on sailing ships for climbing up the rigging. They are light and flexible, and can be stored away when not in use.

**Points: 20**

## MARITIME FLAG

Mariners display flags on board ship as a way of communicating. There are strict rules about how the flags are used.

### SHIP'S WHEEL

**Points: 20**

A wheel is used to steer a ship by altering the position of the rudder.

**Points: 15**

### ANCHOR

When a ship is moored, a heavy anchor lowered overboard on a chain or cable stops it from being moved along by the sea.

### PIRATE FLAG

**Points: 20**
double with answer

This distinctive flag was flown by pirate ships in the early 18th century to show they were about to attack.

*What is the name of the skull and crossbones flag?*

**FIGUREHEAD**

Points: 50 Top Spot!

50

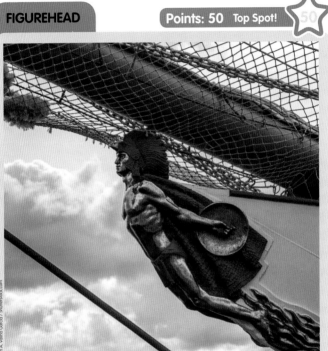

Juan A. Valino Garcia / Shutterstock.com

From the 1500s through to the late 1800s most sailing ships would have a large wooden figure on their bow as a good luck charm to see the sailors safely through their voyage. Elaborately carved and colourfully painted, they were often human shaped although animals and mythical beasts were not uncommon. The last British battleship thought to carry one was the HMS *Rodney* which was launched in 1884.

## SPINNING WHEEL

**Points: 40**

Before the Industrial Revolution began in about 1760, many people had these simple machines in their homes. They used them for spinning sheep's wool into yarn.

**Points: 50**   **Top Spot!**

## WEAVING LOOM

During the Industrial Revolution big factory mills were built to house the newly invented weaving looms, which were used to make textiles.

## SEWING MACHINE

**Points: 30**

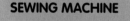

The invention of the sewing machine meant that items of clothing could be made much more quickly than they were by hand.

**Points: 20**

## MANGLE

A mangle used to be an essential part of the laundry. It was used to squeeze water out of hand-washed clothes, which helped them to dry more quickly.

## STEAM ENGINE

**Points: 30**

A steam engine uses the steam from boiling water to create power. Its invention allowed huge advances to be made in machinery for use in farming, industry and transport.

*Name the Scottish engineer associated with the first steam engines. Score 10 points*

**Points: 50**   **Top Spot!**

## PRINTING PRESS

Books, newspapers and posters could all be mass-produced once the printing press had been invented.

## SEXTANT

**Points: 25**

Sextants were used by ships' navigators to determine their latitude and longitude. They work by measuring the angular distance between celestial objects, such as a star and the moon or sun.

**Points: 25**

## TYPEWRITER

Before personal computers were invented, formal letters and documents had to be typed on a typewriter.

*Look out for these items which are made of metal.*

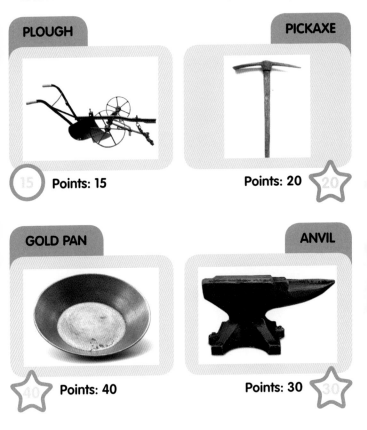

**PLOUGH**

Points: 15

**PICKAXE**

Points: 20

**GOLD PAN**

Points: 40

**ANVIL**

Points: 30

## FOUR-POSTER BED

**Points: 20**

The curtains around these beds were drawn at night to keep people warm while they slept.

**Points: 10**

## KITCHEN RANGE

These massive cookers had several separate ovens used for cooking different things.

## Points: 5

## FRAMED PHOTOGRAPH

Most houses contain a framed photograph of someone or something.

## BABY CRADLE

## Points: 15

Old fashioned cradles stood on curved rockers so the baby could be rocked to sleep.

## Points: 10
double with answer

## LONGCASE CLOCK

These tall clocks contain a long, weighted pendulum that swings from side to side. This allows them to keep the time very accurately.

*What is the popular names for this type of clock?*

A polished wooden writing desk was an essential piece of furniture in any fine house.

Points: 5

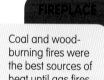

Coal and wood-burning fires were the best sources of heat until gas fires and central heating became available.

Before sewage systems were introduced, many people didn't really have a toilet as such and had to squat over a pot or a pit in the ground. Even those who could afford a 'toilet' tended to have little more than a stone seat with a hole in the bottom. After a while these stone seats were switched for more comfortable wooden chairs with a bucket beneath. Score points for any type of toilet on display.

*See if you can spot these different types of pot.*

**TEAPOT**

Points: 10

**CHAMBER POT**

Points: 15

**COFFEE POT**

Points: 20

**COOKING POT**

Points: 5

**Points: 20**

## EGYPTIAN COFFIN

When they died, Ancient Egyptians were mummified and laid to rest in a series of nested wooden coffins. These were then encased in an outer sarcophagus made of stone.

*Score double points if it contains a mummy.*

volkova natalia / Shutterstock.com

## EGYPTIAN HIEROGLYPHS

**Points: 15**

These are the characters used in Ancient Egyptian writing. They were carved onto stone or written with ink onto a kind of paper made from papyrus plants.

## RECONSTRUCTED SETTLEMENT

Ms Jane Campbell / Shutterstock.com

Reconstructed Stone Age and Iron Age houses allow us to look back in time and see how our ancestors lived.

Points: 10

## POTTERY FRAGMENT

Archaeologists often uncover bits of broken pottery in the ground. If they are lucky, they will find enough fragments to piece the whole pot together.

15 **Points: 15**

## ANCIENT COIN

Score points for any coin from the Roman Empire or from ancient Egypt or Greece.

## TORC

**Points: 50**   Top Spot!   50

A torc was a metal ring worn around the neck as decoration. They were worn during the Bronze Age and also by Celts and Romans during the Iron Age.

40 **Points: 40**

## BROOCH

There were no buttons or zips during ancient times, so people used metal brooches to hold their clothes together.

61

## ROMAN MOSAIC

**Points: 40**

Tiny coloured tiles were arranged into mosaic patterns on the floors of Roman buildings. The more important the building, the more elaborate the pattern.

# INDEX

**Answers: P14** Tree Rings; Dendrochronology. **P18** Space Suit; Neil Armstrong. **P25** Medal: The Victoria Cross; Jolly Roger. **P51** Steam Engine; James Watt. **P55** Longcase Clock; Grandfather Clock.

# i-SPY

How to get your i-SPY certificate and badge

Let us know when you've become a super-spotter with 1000 points and we'll send you a special certificate and badge!

## HERE'S WHAT TO DO!

- ✓ Ask an adult to check your score.

- ✓ Visit www.collins.co.uk/i-SPY to apply for your certificate. If you are under the age of 13 you will need a parent or guardian to do this.

- ✓ We'll send your certificate via email and you'll receive a brilliant badge through the post!